Cheeky Worries

For Wilbur and Noah (AS)
For the dreamers (PD)

First published in Great Britain in 2022 by Jessica Kingsley Publishers
An imprint of Hodder & Stoughton Ltd
An Hachette Company

1

A CIP catalogue record for this title is available from the British Library and the Library of Congress

ISBN 978 1 83997 211 9
eISBN 978 1 83997 212 6

Printed and bound in China by Leo Paper Products Ltd

Jessica Kingsley Publishers' policy is to use papers that
are natural, renewable and recyclable products and made
from wood grown in sustainable forests. The logging
and manufacturing processes are expected to conform
to the environmental regulations of the country of origin.

Jessica Kingsley Publishers
Carmelite House
50 Victoria Embankment
London EC4Y 0DZ

www.jkp.com

Cheeky Worries

A Story to Help Children Talk About and Manage
Scary Thoughts and Everyday Worries

Patrick Davey and Anna Smith
Illustrated by Anne Wilson

Jessica Kingsley Publishers
London and Philadelphia

This is a story about Finn.

Finn is a normal boy, just like any other.

Finn likes sliding... *wheeee!*

Finn likes
adventures...
ooooh!

Finn likes
parties...
boooogie!

One day, Finn
was on the bus to school.
Finn loves to sit right at
the front and pretend he is
the driver.

Suddenly, something
strange happened.

A scary thought popped into his head.

WHAT IF MUMMY GETS OFF THE BUS WITHOUT ME?

Finn felt butterflies in his tummy and his heart started beating faster.

He felt scared.

He stopped playing and held on to his mummy's hand until they got off the bus, and he forgot the scary thought.

That night it
happened again.

He had another
scary thought.

WHAT IF THERE
IS A MONSTER
UNDER MY BED?

Finn felt scared.

He did not want
to go to bed.

The next day, Finn went to the park.

He loves the park, but most of all he loves
the yellow slide.

As he sat at the top,
it happened again.

WHAT IF I SLIP AND FALL OFF THE SLIDE?

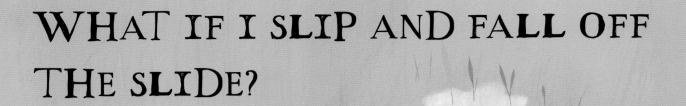

Finn felt scared and climbed off the slide.

Finn sat down on a bench.

He felt sad.

Suddenly there was a *whoosh* as a big, fluffy owl swooped down and perched next to him.

'Greetings, Finn,
I am the wise owl. I have come
to see you because I know your thoughts have
made you feel scared and have stopped you doing
things you like.' The owl put her soft wing around
him and carried on talking.

'Scary thoughts can seem very frightening.
I know about them because lots of people have them.
They even have a name: cheeky worries.'

'Cheeky worries.
Why do you call them that?'
Finn asked.

'Because they sneak into your thoughts without asking. They make you feel scared, they don't always tell the truth and they can stop you doing the things you want to do.'

'What can I do when I have a cheeky worry?'
asked Finn. The owl smiled and blinked
her big, wise eyes.

'Well, there are lots of things you can do.
First, you have to spot the cheeky worry.'

'Like on the slide, when I had a cheeky worry about slipping?' Finn said.

'Or when I was on the bus and was worried that Mummy might leave me there?'

'Yes, yes, that's right. Well done!' said the owl.

'Now you've spotted your cheeky worries, it may help to tell someone about them.'

Finn looked thoughtful and said,

'So, I can say: *Mummy, I'm having a cheeky worry about monsters under my bed?*'

'Yes, that's right. Telling a grown-up about a cheeky worry can make it seem less frightening,' said the owl.

'Don't forget, Finn, we call them cheeky worries because they trick us by telling us that something bad is going to happen, and it doesn't!

Your cheeky worries tell you that there is a monster under your bed, but you've never seen one, have you?'

Finn thought for a while. The owl was right. He had never seen a monster under his bed!

Finn slowly realised that although they felt scary and real, his cheeky worries had never come true.

He had never fallen off the slide.

And he had never been left on the bus.

38

Finn gasped. 'So they are cheeky because they try and trick me!'

'Yes,' said the owl, 'and because we know that they trick you, it means that you don't need to pay attention to what they say.

It might help to say:
Hello cheeky worry,
I'm too busy playing
to listen to you.'

'Wow, I can do that myself,' said Finn.
'If I have a cheeky worry that Mummy
is going to leave me on the bus I can say:
Hello, cheeky worry.

I'm too busy driving this bus to listen to you.'

'Yes, of course you can, and here is one of
my magic feathers to help you,' the
owl said as she hopped off the bench.

'Thank you,' said Finn, who noticed that other feathers were missing from the owl.

'Why are you missing so
many magic feathers?'
asked Finn.

The wise owl beat her
broad wings, began to
gently lift off the ground
and turned to look back.

'Because, Finn, my brave little friend, everybody – however big or small – has cheeky worries.'

It was then that Finn saw a feather tucked under his dad's cap, another poking out the top of his friend's welly boot and one in the park keeper's shirt pocket.

Finn smiled and started running towards his favourite yellow slide, shouting, 'Sorry, cheeky worry, I'm too busy sliding to listen to you!'

And he played happily in the park until it was time to go home for tea.

The End

Guide for Grown-Ups

Cheeky Worries aims to give children and their caregivers a shared language through which to navigate their emotional worlds. The story is used as a means to share evidence-based psychological approaches to managing worries. It aims to simplify the ideas behind these methods so that children can learn skills to manage their emotional experiences and caregivers can develop the confidence to help them do so.

Cognitive behavioural approaches to anxiety consider how our appraisals of a situation can lead to particular feelings which, in turn, can lead to certain behaviours. The story helps children understand how their appraisal of a situation, for example: *What if I slip and fall off the slide*, may lead to anxious feelings in their bodies and consequent avoidance – in this instance, getting off the slide or not going on it again. Children may not necessarily have the language to express these kinds of ideas to their caregivers and may just refuse to do something, or express their anxiety as physical pain.

To help children become resilient adults we want them to develop an understanding of what anxiety is and how it makes them feel in their bodies. Most importantly, we want them to understand that, although anxiety can feel unpleasant, it isn't dangerous, and it doesn't need to get in the way of them having a full life. Moreover, it is something experienced by everyone and it's OK to talk about it. Learning skills to navigate emotional experiences is similar to learning any other skill, such as tying a shoelace or telling the time.

How Does *Cheeky Worries* Help?

Normalising

Cheeky Worries shows children that anxiety is normal and everyone feels this way at times. Finn learns that he is not alone in experiencing it.

Shared language

Cheeky Worries provides a language that children can connect with and use to communicate a set of experiences to their caregiver. In the book, the wise owl talks to Finn about his cheeky worries and gives him a way to put a name to what he is feeling.
  Helpful practice:

- Once you have read the book together you could ask your child if they have ever had a cheeky worry, and share some of your own.

- If a child seems upset and is struggling to express what they are feeling, it may be helpful to check if they are having a cheeky worry.

- We have been told by parents that their children sometimes request to read *Cheeky Worries* if they are struggling with something. Perhaps use their request as an opportunity to explore whether they are having any cheeky worries.

Validation

The wise owl provides guidance on how to respond to cheeky worries. Our inclination can be to dismiss or reassure when children feel anxious, but it is crucial that their feelings and experiences are heard and validated. The wise owl models responses that caregivers can use to help children develop skills to manage their anxiety.
  Helpful responses when a child expresses anxiety or a cheeky worry:

- That sounds so scary – thank you for telling me. Would you like to talk more about it?

- That sounds like a cheeky worry. How is it making you feel inside your body?

- What would the wise owl say?

Tackling avoidance

Children may often want to avoid activities that make them feel anxious, even if they normally enjoy them. Finn learns that feeling anxious and worried doesn't have to lead to avoidance of activities that will bring him joy – by understanding that the worries are trying to trick him, Finn discovers that even though anxious thoughts can be frightening, he does not need to let them affect his behaviour.

Helpful questions if a child seems reluctant to do something they may normally enjoy:

- Are you having cheeky worries about going on the slide?

- Are your cheeky worries telling you something bad is going to happen?

- Is there anything that you're worried is going to happen?

The language of cheeky worries

By calling anxious thoughts cheeky worries, children are introduced to the idea that, although they may have worries and anxious thoughts, these aren't facts or accurate predictions of how things will turn out. Caregivers can help children see that the worries aren't necessarily true and, as such, children can acknowledge them but don't need to listen to what the thoughts are predicting will happen. Caregivers can begin to explore the outcome of the predictions to consolidate the idea that the anxious predictions don't come true:

- It sounds like you're having a cheeky worry. We know that cheeky worries can try to trick you – do you think your worry is tricking you now?

- Let's find out later if your cheeky worry was trying to trick you.

Sometimes all a child needs in order to feel better is to know that someone else understands, or to realise that what they are feeling is normal, and the experience of sharing their worries can make them feel much more manageable.

We hope that *Cheeky Worries* will help.

Patrick and Anna

Dr Patrick Davey

After completing a psychology degree at Cardiff University, Patrick went on to study a Postgraduate Diploma in Broadcast Journalism. He worked as a BBC journalist before he hung up his microphone and became a care worker for adults with autism. He went on to study medicine at Southampton University, after which he completed specialist training to become a Consultant Psychiatrist and member of the Royal College of Psychiatrists.

Patrick is passionate about community mental health provision and exploring better ways to offer early support to our population. Beyond his clinical work, he is an NHS clinical entrepreneur and has recently launched MOAI Health, a mental health and wellbeing digital platform for organisations.

Patrick is a huge advocate of the power of play, connection and belonging. He loves improvised drama, any sport, cheddar cheese and dogs.

Dr Anna Smith

Anna studied psychology at the University of Nottingham and completed her professional doctorate in Clinical Psychology at Kings College London. She then went on to do a Postgraduate Diploma in Cognitive Behavioural Therapy and has completed additional training in Compassion Focused Therapy.

Anna has worked in a variety of clinical settings, including specialist anxiety clinics for children, and has experience managing a national specialist service for adults with treatment-resistant anxiety disorders.

Anna lives in London with her two sons, both of whom have plenty of cheeky worries! Noticing that her four year old had some anxieties about getting on the bus inspired Anna to come up with ways to talk to him about what he was thinking and feeling. Anna and her boys enjoy playing football and cricket, watching films together and making sure that cheeky worries don't get in the way of having a good time!

Also available: *How to Help Children Manage Cheeky Worries*

How to Help Children Manage Cheeky Worries is an online video course designed for teachers and parents who want to better support children with their cheeky worries. It guides you step-by-step through the principles of helping children to share and manage their worries and shows how these principles and evidence-based techniques can be applied to help in different scenarios and with different common worries. It answers FAQs about managing worries and anxiety and features printable worksheets for children. The course has been developed by Patrick Davey and Anna Smith in consultation with parents and schools.

Find out more at library.jkp.com.

Read more books from JKP

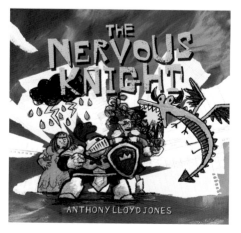